HEALTH CARE ABC'S :

A Primer to Understand & Navigate Health CARE

Bette A. Grey, BA RRT CPFT

Long Lake Publishers

The characters and events portrayed in this book are true to the best knowledge of the author.

ISBN-13: 979-8-9969256-8-1 (Ebook)
ISBN-13: 979-8-9969256-7-4 (paperback)
ISBN-13: 979-8-9969256-9-8 (hardcover)

first edition 2026
10 9 8 7 6 5 4 3 2 1
manuscript in Garamond 12pt

Library of Congress Control Number:
available upon request
Printed in the United States of America

DEDICATION

This book is dedicated to:

My faith and belief in God. He put the right people in my path at the right time so I could use my talents and knowledge to make people's lives just a little better.

Miss Amelia Marie Grey, my granddaughter, whose wisdom is beyond her years. I hope she and her generation will have excellent health CARE in their lifetimes!

CJ for unrelenting encouragement to get it in print. Never stopped believing in me.

All of the patients over the years who allowed me to help them navigate some of the most difficult times of their lives.

TABLE OF CONTENTS

AUTHOR PREFACE

I am an AMERICAN PATIENT IN THE USA: what does that get me in REALITY? A free band aid? Great care?

Does it mean I have ready access to healthcare when I need it? Does it mean that I receive quality healthcare at every step of the way? Does it mean that communication between myself and my providers is straightforward? Does it mean that I receive the best bang for my buck for the healthcare I receive? Does it mean that I can navigate seamlessly through the healthcare systems? Does it mean that I feel safe when I am in a healthcare system? Does it mean that as a woman, my healthcare and attention is the same as my male counterparts? Does it mean that I may or may not lose my house and all my belongings because of having outstanding healthcare debt? Does it mean that if my credit score becomes skewed because of the medical debt that I may not be able to make the life purchases to live? Does it mean that there could be lifesaving treatments that are not accessible to me? Does it mean that as a parent I have to worry about how my special needs child can get services that will make their life so much better?

Does it mean that I have to rely on the kindness of strangers via a crowdfunding site to pay off my medical debt? Does it mean that the same facility where I am receiving healthcare, of which I can't afford, that I can receive "charity care" or uncompensated care?

Does it mean as reimbursements from the federal government get shuffled, does it mean that access begins to shrivel up because healthcare systems are not sustainable?

Does it mean that there will be enough medical providers of all professions for me?

Does it mean that I may have to die needlessly because I can't afford healthcare or healthcare insurance? Does it mean that the services needed to help me die are unavailable?

The answers are "yes" and "no".

At the end of the day, you are like the crème of the sandwich cookie, squeezed by both the healthcare system and the health insurance companies. It doesn't matter if the cookie portion of that sandwich cookie is chocolate, vanilla, strawberry, or lemon - you still are the crème. I don't care if you like to twist the two cookie sides to get to the crème or if you just take a huge chomp out of the cookie, you are still the crème, continuously being squeezed.

This primer is the distillation of decades of being a patient and being a health care provider. I have been an active participant in health care as the patient and have stood on the sidelines as the provider attempting to keep patients breathing better. I want to have this book be a reminder every patient has a voice – please use that voice to get the best care possible. If someone you love has no strength in their own voice, be that voice for them.

My Own Patient Story

I share this story with you because, I too have a story, one that has spanned my lifetime! Even as someone who has medical knowledge, I am not immune to an imperfect healthcare system which should do better and be better!

With a chronic disease that went undiagnosed for most of my life, I mucked and mired my way through more rabbit holes than you could shake a stick at. Bringing the same complaints to every one of my medical providers over the years, where they were categorized in a handy dandy diagnoses list which probably were only reviewed sporadically. Nobody ever put together all of my patient chart notes and said, "Gee, she has this same complaint over and over!" Instead they sent me to a lot of testing, some of which was unpleasant. Those tests cost my insurance companies thousands of dollars and myself lots of co-pays. Had only ONE medical provider looked at my body habitus, in other words looked at my whole body as a complete unit, they would have seen how disproportionate my body truly was. It took only ONE provider to notice my ankle swelling, which then set the opening of Pandora's box as to why I had the same complaints over and over. I don't like using the "gender" card, but the disease, LIPEDEMA, is a gender disease. It rarely affects males. In this country, if your BMI (body mass index) is on the high side and you may look "fat", then you are advised to lose weight. If I had a dollar for every person who told me that I just needed to eat less and exercise more, I would be somewhat wealthy. I was essentially 'cookie-cuttered', meaning I had a specific BMI that fit into the category of obese. My assumption always was that even though I told providers that I didn't eat a half gallon of ice cream or a dozen donuts at a setting; they chose to not believe me. As I look back over this disease that is literally taking me out at my knees now, I wonder if things had been different, would I have ended up with this same outcome. Medical schools and other professional schools need to get better at teaching their tutelages about the body whole, meaning that humans are not meant to be just a conglomeration of differential diagnoses, check lists, and laboratory tests. Quality health care starts with listening to the patient, comparing notes, and then using the multifaceted checklists to come up with an answer for your patient. In my case, most of my providers were sincere in their attempts to help me feel better, but they never went that one step above. They listened to my spin of stories and of course understanding health care, the discussions were more of a professional to a professional rather than patient to provider. I am often reminded there needs to be a separation of patient from health care provider.

What I intend to do throughout this primer is to offer simple but proven tips and hope they will serve as empowerment tools! The stories I present are true stories, with patients' names changed. They are a smattering of the thousands of patients' journeys I was fortunate to be a part of.

Remember as a patient, you are unique! Sadly, your story is occasionally like many others in these United States, tragic and unconscionable.

PATIENT INFORMATION

Full Name: ____________________

Date of Birth: ____________________

Blood Type: ____________________

Medicare ID Number: ____________________

Secondary Insurance Name/ID#

____

Medicaid ID Number:____________________

Secondary Medicaid Provider:

____

ID Number:____________________

Private Insurance Provider :

____

ID Number:____________________

Group ID Number____________________

Phone # (usually the back of the card):

____

Pharmacy name:____________________

Phone #:____________________

Location of Medical History Files:

____

____

Medication History:

Date started	Medication/dose	Date ended

ALLERGIES:

____

____

____

____

HISTORY - Surgeries/Illnesses

Date	Description

Primary Care Provider: ____________________________

Phone ____________________________

Email ____________________________

Primary Dentist: ____________________________

Phone ____________________________

Email ____________________________

Emergency Contact: ____________________________

Phone ____________________________

Email ____________________________

Other Contact ________________________________

Phone ______________________________

Other Contact: ___________________________________

Phone _______________________________

NOTES:

STATE OF AMERICAN HEALTH CARE

Pulling medical insurance at some of the most crucial times in a person's life is barbaric. In fact, it is downright unconscionable. But it doesn't stop in this country. It's not unusual for health insurance premiums and benefits to change at the drop of the actuarial hat or data analyses, along with the values of KPI (key performance indicators). In the health insurance industry, is success based on the ability of a patient to actually use the insurance and not be bankrupted, or is it based on the bottom line of how much the company is profiting from the people it supposedly serves?

For those on government funded health insurance such as Medicaid, renewals are a part of everyone's life in order to maintain their insurance. Often times with one small change in one of the requested pieces of information, folks lose their Medicaid at the push of a computer button. Many tend to accept their fate in life and not question why. They are thrown into the vat of the uninsured with many having chronic diseases that with their coverage were under control. Left unchecked, their medical conditions worsen, causing them to receive even more extensive healthcare services. Or if they refuse to get care because they know they cannot afford it, they simply yet again face their fate being death!

The harshness continues as folks have to understand every nook and cranny of what happens with their health insurance. With the business of life, I am not ever sure how anyone can keep up. Back in the day, patients would actually get a booklet of benefits, now employers direct their employees to query an online portal to get their benefits. Some people are not technologically savvy and cannot navigate. Most benefit booklets are multiple pages, therein lies yet another obstacle to getting access to what the benefits cover. Why do we make these lifesaving things so much harder? An employee is fortunate to have anyone in HR who understands the benefits the employer may offer. And if they do or don't, they often refer the employee to the health insurance company. They in a sense don't want to be responsible for giving inaccurate advice.

In their infinite wisdom and somewhat cowardice, our elected officials who reside in Congress, have put even bigger obstacles in place by approving HR Bill-1. Be reminded, Congress all receives quite the best healthcare benefits in the country, not like our citizen Medicare, Medicaid or commercial based insurance. With the stroke of the Presidential pen and the votes of Congress, subsidies for the ACA beneficiaries were wiped out and not addressed; Medicaid and Medicare rules have changed, and funding and reimbursements for hospitals have taken a hit. As citizens die because of their decisions, Congress can pick up the phone and have the best state of the art healthcare. The taxpayers who fund their healthcare through their tax dollars often have to wait months to even get primary care appointments. It becomes clearly self-evident that the government has no interest in helping folks remain alive and productive. Sounds harsh. It is meant to be harsh and it is the reality of the country in which we live.

Healthcare coverage is like gold to most people, without it they decline to seek care, including preventive care. Where does that all get us: it gets us to more over capacity emergency rooms and much more expensive medical bills. If folks of this country were given basic healthcare, including labs (which cost pennies on the dollar), these same labs could alert a medical provider to possible impending medical issues; blood pressure checks; solid consistent nutrition education; and vaccines. But the same old song and dance is played over and over in the government houses and at the White House: "THERE IS NOT ENOUGH MONEY!" Give me a break, we fund plenty of frivolous things in this country. Unfortunately, we need to change the tune for the song and dance to something where we value the citizens' lives in this country.

The United States for all of its medical finesse and technology, we have some very dismal outcomes, like infant and maternal mortality. At least $100 billion, that's billion with a B, is spent annually on unnecessary tests, malpractice lawsuits, and inadequate care. With that being said, one in three patients will have less than stellar outcomes.

American healthcare stopped being "caring" when the system required folks to carry plastic insurance cards for primary care visits. What's the difference between "healthcare" and "health care"? I remind myself on a daily basis, there is a difference, although we keep trying to lump the two terms together. In my estimation, along with many other people who have been party to giving care, "healthcare" refers to the business side of healthcare, whereas "health care" is truly the art and act of caring about the humans you are interacting with in order to make them well! Wow, could you imagine if we made wellness a priority?! If we stopped being a country of always sick care, what would that mean for the pharmaceutical companies, hospital systems, and health insurance companies? Would it mean their profit margins would decrease, hmmm, just thinking out loud here, but is that why wellness is NOT truly a priority? If wellness were a priority, medical providers would be handing out more prescriptions which tell their patients to eat better, move a little more, get some sleep, turn off the electronic devices, etc. As we all know, prescriptions are generally filled and we follow the instructions on the bottle of medications. If we as patients were given a prescription for wellness, would we follow the instructions like those on the prescription bottle? A prescription is a prescription is a prescription.

WELLNESS IS NOT PROFITABLE TO THOSE WHOSE BUSINESS IS "SICK CARE"!

Let that sink in for a bit! "Health" care vs "Sick" care.

Growing up in the 60's and 70's before health insurance companies got into providing coverage for these services, I or my family always paid cash for any medical visits. Most of the time, not only did you get "hands on" evaluations, but you may have gotten an injection and/or a packet of medications that the provider had in his possession at the time. Most of the medical providers also would do house calls for some of their sickest patients to keep them out of the hospitals and emergency rooms.

Were the medical providers back then wealthy, probably not, but they loved their patients like their own family. In lieu of money, they would accept a chicken, a loaf of bread or anything else the patient had to offer. In today's world, medical providers could get to know their patients at this level, but often due to the time constraints dictated by the corporate business world of seeing a patient every 9-10 minutes - it becomes extremely difficult. And in today's world, one complaint per visit is the maximum - the typical response when you try to trot out more than one (and only one), you are often told to come back.

I have become increasingly aware that medical providers do less and less 'hands on' evaluations. Yet in the electronic medical record, they document their findings as 'normal'. They may not listen to your heart and lungs, but yet document that the lung sounds and heart sounds are A-Ok. I believe the pressure to get folks through the system like cattle going to slaughter is the reason we keep taking shortcuts. I was always reminded as a respiratory therapist that if you "hadn't performed a task", don't document that you did. Those sage words should be spread far and wide in today's medical care climate.

How do we get back on track?

Does it mean we have to stop treating healthcare as a business and get back to what it should really be - caring for patients as a whole, not just body parts?

Does it mean that each individual in America is educated from the time they are able to read about how to be healthy and well? It is done in other countries, their citizens are taught from the get-go about health and wellness. Our country pretends to teach youngsters about health, but falls short. If we were doing a great job at that, wouldn't their be fewer youngsters who could be classified as obese; wouldn't there be less worriment about the mental health status of kiddos, many of whom are medicated at a young age for anxiety and depression; wouldn't the Gross Domestic Product (GDP) be less than what it is currently, around 20 percent, meaning $1 out of every $5 goes to some type of healthcare spending; wouldn't we have fewer adults with diabetes, high blood pressure, COPD; on and on? Simple solutions like teaching and showing kiddos: how to put together a healthy plate of food, how to understand what sugar does and actually showing them where sugars are hidden, why spending so much time on their screens is truly detrimental to their health (sitting is the new smoking), teaching them coping skills that work, getting them to understand that STD's are real, teaching them vaping is dangerous.....there's a hundred more things like this. If this country focused on wellness and starting this education at a very young age, healthcare in America could mirror the wellness statistics of other countries.

Does it mean that we address our food supply and put stronger requirements for better food quality in place? We'll use wheat and flour as a primary example. Many Americans cannot tolerate the wheat they ingest. Since the American diet is heavily laden with carbohydrates that use flour, Americans ingest a lot of wheat. Wheat that may be tainted with pesticides other countries stopped using decades ago. True stories, Americans who go abroad to places like Italy, can eat volumes of wheat in the form of pasta and pastries, and suffer no ill effects. Yet in the states, they find themselves in misery after eating any type of wheat products grown here. Why are we not more diligent in getting things out of our food supply that are harmful? Just like much else in healthcare, it is always about profits and profitability!

Profits and profitability keep Americans fighting the 'sick' battle! Until we begin to push back and say enough is enough, our GDP will continue to rise; we will continue to accept our healthcare as it is, versus what it really could be; and death will continue to be the only option for many. Dismal isn't it?! But it doesn't have to be, you can take charge of your own health and wellness! You, the human, has to have skin in the game by deciding if you want to be healthy or sick! You have to decide to speak up about the cost of your health insurance premiums - is it really acceptable the costs go up and you get less bang for your buck? We have all heard the adage "the squeaky wheel gets the most grease", well if the people in charge of those increases never hear from the people they are affecting, then they may just believe everyone is A-OK with those increases. We can ask our schools to implement better health and wellness curriculums, maybe even ask for a much more hands-on approach to health and wellness (wouldn't that be a great pilot project to fund?). We can write to those companies who process and grow our food and tell them **they need to DO BETTER** by us all and there are no excuses, **NONE, for not doing better**!

I would remind everyone, that all of us will probably wear a label of "patient" at some point in our lives. Few of us leave this planet without having been a patient at some point during our tenure here. I would also encourage everyone to advocate for themselves! Believe it or not you can do it! You can speak up and ask pointed questions, understand that your own perseverance and voice can change the health care you receive, and that you have some control over being well or being sick!

THE BOTTOM UP APPROACH: EMPOWERING PATIENTS

This book is my attempt to work from the trenches upward, giving patients tools they may need to be able to advocate for themselves. My goal is to educate folks in a simplistic manner, in order that they may be able to have meaningful conversations across the health care spectrum. This is not astrophysics.

I have spent many many hours navigating both health insurance and health care. And when I say hours and hours, my life span has probably been decreased by days, if not months or years for the amount of time spent doing just that. Time spent on the phone (on hold A LOT); time writing letters; time meeting with folks in person, etc.

They have always said time is relative, but in the American healthcare system time is life. The proverbial "time is money" can be self-evident especially when you lose precious wages trying to jump through multiple hoops to get the right answers. Sometimes, the time spent navigating means not having those precious moments to spend on getting well! If you are fortunate, you will have someone who can help follow the bouncing balls, which translates into getting a reasonable resolution.

I know that many people think their problem may be unique unto themselves, I am here to disagree with those thoughts. You would be surprised how many folks find themselves walking through the vast wasteland of health-care navigation with a problem very similar to yours. Exponentially for every one person who is facing the same issue, there are at least nine or ten more.

Why why why does this have to be this hard? Actually, it doesn't have to be this hard. By modernizing and computerizing health care, it should be simpler. The old method of using paper charts always ran the risk of losing a pertinent piece of information if a page from the chart was lost. But in reality, now we have multiple tools at our fingertips, including the genesis and development of artificial intelligence (AI), which has great potential to help the already harried medical providers.

Continuity of care relies on not only the information contained in the chart, but also the ability of anyone reading it to critically think about what all the information means. I long for the days when folks in health care use critical thinking like they use hand sanitizer, applying it liberally multiple times a day!

Patients often think they do not know what the right words are to say which helps anyone on the other end of the phone line or computer inbox understand their issues. **COMMUNICATION IS THE ABSOLUTE KEY** to not only navigation but also to getting the best bang for your buck when it comes to the care received. As you read through the tips the word "ASK" will be front and center - there has never been a better word! People are often afraid to ask, fearing the answer is only ever going to be "NO"! You may be surprised the answer isn't always "NO"! You will never know unless you ASK! I remind people you don't know what you don't know until you NEED to know it!

Even though 'insurance' may 'cover' a lot of services being done, those dollars are your dollars, whether in the forms of insurance premiums, co-pays, or deductibles. From the bottom-up, we might just improve the American health care systems by educating folks on 'how to be a patient' !

LET THE EMPOWERMENT BEGIN: SIMPLE TIPS TO NAVIGATE

Advocacy

Tip #1 I AM THE PATIENT!!

Remember, REMEMBER, *Remember* you are the patient. It is your body. Do not be bullied by anyone into having a procedure done, taking a medication, etc. **ASK QUESTIONS** and do your research. Research doesn't always come by way of Dr Google either. It should come from an extensive give and take with the provider providing the options. The optimal word is "should". With the advent of AI, discernment will become SO important in differentiating truth vs misinformation.

Tip #2 Patient advocates looking from the inside out.

Many healthcare systems have patient advocates embedded in their employee fleet. They may be known by different names including patient liaison. The best way to reach them is to **ask the hospital operator to speak with this staff person**. More often than not, you will get their voicemail. Don't let that be daunting. Leave a clear concise message. They will get back to you. Never leave emergency type messages on their voicemail system. Emergency issues need to be addressed with the nursing or physician supervisors. Patient advocates don't only address the care issues. They have been known to track down someone's dentures that were lost. If those dentures are never found, the hospital has a system in place which can provide reimbursement to replace them. Likewise for glasses, wallets, jewelry. If you are concerned about your personal belongings, either leave them home or hand them off to someone who you trust.

Tip #3 BE KIND TO YOUR HEALTH CARE PROVIDER, they are human just like you!

I know there are a lot more patients than medical providers. Yes, for anyone listening or reading this, medical providers are not mechanical machines that go 24x7x365. Robots haven't taken over our care completely yet, as of this writing. Remember your health care provider may have a family, a medical disease, may have IBF (Insurance Battling Fatigue - I think this term could be used as part of the medical coding!), aging parents who need care, etc. Medical providers battle some of the same wars that we as patients do. They are also like sponges—they absorb every story, every diagnosis, every death. Most find positive alternative ways like gardening, farming, reading, golfing, needlepoint, and hobbies to counterbalance a lot of the negative things that happen in health care. However, some providers have a difficult time coping with what's been happening over the years and they decide to end their lives. Why would I add medical provider suicide to a book about how to navigate health care? Because as the business of medicine has become just atrocious and unmanageable, I believe that those who care for us are expected to be like robots, treat patient after patient, maybe thirty or forty in a day. Many times we start at the crack of dawn with the crowing of the rooster and don't end until the streetlights have come on. Imagine working those hours day after day, month after month, year after year, with little self-care time. It can catch up in a hurry to send their mental health down a spiral. The business of healthcare has only added more stressors, as the medical providers have to deal with denials of things they know are appropriate to keep their patients alive and well!

Most medical providers know what they are signing up for when they enter the auspicious halls of health care. But even the toughest of the most stoic sometimes hit bumps in the road that just throw them for the proverbial loop. One of their favorite patients die; they have to give a cancer diagnosis to five patients in a row; their own family experiences issues, on and on and on - THEY ARE HUMAN BEINGS, please, please, please treat them as such. Maybe even ask them, "how are you doing today?" at your next appointment!

Tip #4 It's all about the alphabet soup!

There are so many acronyms bandied about in health care. Some are just made up to fit into the healthcare system's work arounds. If someone starts rattling off the acronyms and/or initials, with your own ears having a tough time catching up, **ask the person** expounding on these acronyms to **STOP** and explain exactly what they are saying. Never be afraid that you may come off as being 'stupid' if you ask for an explanation. The explanation should be easy to understand.

Tip #5 Most healthcare CEO's do care about the care!

You would be interested to know that CEO's of healthcare organizations do really care about the care that is being given under their leadership. The problem is, it's very hard to have access to them to even start to understand that point of view. Yes, one could say that they 'should' care because they make an exceptional amount of money to do just that. They have multiple bosses in the form of a board of directors. I have had the opportunity to work with several CEO's about issues within their healthcare systems. For the most part, they want to know the issues. They can't address what they have no idea about.

If you want to get in touch with a CEO - the easiest way is to call the hospital or facility operator. Ask them to transfer you to the Administration Department. Someone in the department can direct you to the CEO. I have written letters to CEO's. For the most part, they do respond with answers.

Don't ever think that you are "just" the patient. Be reminded that without patients, there is no facility, therefore no CEO! Again, always be polite and kind! Explain the situation with as much information as possible - it's the only way they can make any type of informed comments.

The Basics

Tip #6 OPEN THE MAIL!

Open all mail coming in from any healthcare system or health insurance company.

The mail is not your enemy. In fact, it is your FRIEND!

The mail allows you to understand what is owed or what is NOT owed. It keeps you out of the financial collections world. The collections folks will turn your life upside down and they will shake you out until they recoup what is supposedly owed! Therefore, open the mail and know for sure what they are talking about, then and only then can you fight!!

Remember most medical billing goes out very shortly after any services you may have had done. It doesn't mean the bills are correct, it just means they are now headed towards your inbox or mailbox.

Side note - if you receive emails, create a separate folder for them, **NAME THE EMAIL FOLDER** something based on the reminder it is regarding your healthcare!

Tip #7 Patient portals.

Patient portals can be either a blessing or a curse! Since it has become harder and harder to get past the gatekeeper of your medical provider's office; there needs to be a way to at least try to get a message to them. Not only is the portal important for exchanging messages, but it is also home to a lot of your medical and billing history, appointments, and diagnostic testing results.

Since patient portals have arrived in the health care arena, patients use them consistently. For every good idea, there eventually becomes a negative side to that idea. Well, that is the case for patient portals. For instance, in a medical practice with ten thousand (10,000) patients, if a hundred patients decide to send a message on any given day; wowsa that's a lot of computer traffic. No medical provider can read every message, therefore they usually can go through *a filtering process*.

Keeping in mind you are not the only patient to send a message—**the best option is to be very concise** about what you want to say. Do NOT write "War and Peace". A couple of lines is sufficient. If you can't write less than "War and Peace", just send a message that reads:

"I am having issues with.......... Would someone from your office be able to call me?" "Please and Thanks!"

A message like the above would get 'triaged' to a staff member. The staff member then can call you so you can elaborate about what the issue you are experiencing might be. Once there is more information shared, the medical staff can formulate a plan with your provider's input. It may sound simplistic, but a problem is created if any one of the loops doesn't get completed. If that happens, your provider may never know about your message and can't evaluate what you may need. Too often, you may otherwise get the message, "Go to the ER!"

Please know that you should never send an urgent message to the portal! Be mindful, if there is not a timely reply back to your message, don't wait to seek further care if your symptoms are changing for the worst. Some patients wait, thinking there might be a message coming soon, and continue to feel worse and worse, until they *have* to find urgent/emergent care.

The other possible concern about the portal is the release of medical results into your chart. A lot of times if there is an issue with the results, people go into panic mode. They then seek out "Dr. Google". Depending on how you post your question there, you may fear you have a terminal disease. In reality, it could be less dire, if you understand how all of the pieces of the puzzle fit together.

Tip #8 Always Review Your *OFFICIAL* Medical Records!

Medical records are like fingerprints, they should be unique to you the patient. Understanding and keeping up with what is in them is paramount to a great healthcare journey. As you watch at most healthcare appointments, the provider generally points and clicks all of their answers to what is happening to you at the appointment. For instance, they may click that your heart and lungs are clear, but have never listened to your chest at the visit. In the world of computer technology, it has become very easy to do the 'point and click' thing. Remember that your medical provider may retire, die, or move away, which means it is extremely important to have correct medical records to hand off to the next medical provider. Although the medical records may just be parked, as in the electronic chart and really nobody has taken a "good" look at them, they are there for your new provider to be do their due diligence in clarifying information.

On that same note, always ALWAYS, *always* make a copy of your medical records as you get them. If periodically, you review your patient portal, print out any documentation that is found there. Please file them appropriately with your other medical information!

The reason I ask you to review the medical records on a regular basis is the following story! A female patient had the opportunity to review their medical records, only to find out that she had a prostate! Absolute TRUE story! When healthcare becomes fully engaged with AI, it will become even more imperative to know what is in your medical records.

On a different note, if you decide to file a malpractice lawsuit, correct medical records are imperative to mount any type of defense. For instance, if the provider checks off that everything is A-OK, but in reality you know it wasn't—how can any attorney represent you without correct records?!

*my notes:*____

____

Tip #9 Emergency contacts and advance healthcare directives.

Always have someone who can act as your emergency contact, and if possible a couple of folks! Make sure your emergency contacts know at the bare minimum your medical history, allergies, blood type, and medications. They are actually considered a bridge between you and others as your healthcare story begins! It is always wise to give your emergency contact a list of these things (fill out '*Patient Information*' above).

Emergency contacts can be informed of what's happened to you, but they may not always be able to make decisions about your care, unless they are legally named to do so. This is definitely worth paying attention to and deciding who can make difficult decisions in the event you are unconscious and can't make decisions for yourself.

Living wills and determining what level of care you want beyond the immediate medical issue is important. Do you want CPR? Do you want to be put on a ventilator? Would you want a feeding tube to keep you fed and alive? If you develop a horrid infection, do you want antibiotics? What about blood transfusions?

I believe the wisest thing to do is to make everyone aware of your wishes and write them down. Samples of living wills and advance healthcare directives can easily be found on the web. Often times, when you put together your last will and testament, these items along with naming a durable power of attorney are included in the legal package.

*my notes:*____

____

Tip #10 Collect All Bills, Paperwork and Notes in One Place!

In the world of healthcare, it is imperative to create a 'one stop' shop for anything pertaining to your medical records. Find a large folder, a 3-ring binder, anything where you can place medical records, billing, and any other important information that helps you fight the good fight or it at least allows you to have an incredible history of your healthcare journey!

DO NOT just throw things into a folder! **NO! NO! NO!** Organize like things together. In other words, a medical bill should match any medical documentation you may have like an after-visit summary or simply a copy of the medical record.

*my notes:*____

____

Tip #11 Document DOCUMENT *Document*.

Although a lot of the ensuing rules are important, documenting who you talked to about any healthcare issue is absolutely necessary. DATE, TIME, AND THE PERSON YOU SPOKE WITH NEEDS TO BE WRITTEN DOWN WITH ANY ENCOUNTER YOU HAVE. You may get three different answers from three different people. But by having the documented information at your fingertips, you have ammunition for when they say they see nothing in the computer regarding your ask or concern. Add it to your files with the heading in mind, "QUESTIONS ASKED"!

If you don't like or think you are not getting the 'right' answers, ASK FOR A SUPERVISOR! Often a supervisor can look back over the activity of any inquiries over the course of time, whereas the general customer service person answering the call may not be able to.

Most phone calls are 'recorded for quality assurance' purposes. If push comes to shove, you can always ask for them to review their transcripts to ascertain what was said on the phone call. To that point, always, always, always be kind, even if your head feels like it is going to explode at any moment! Keep your cool!

*my notes:*____

____

Health Care People

Tip #12 Hospitalists (WHO?)

Back in the 'golden days' of health care when your doctor would have hospital privileges, meaning if you were admitted, they were in charge of your care. They were the ones who would come to your bedside most every morning. They would chat with you about how you were feeling; any test results; and discharge requirements, etc. With the advent of many independent practitioners either being bought out by larger healthcare systems or conglomerates, hospitalists are now in vogue. They have relieved your primary care practitioner (PCP) of having to visit or care for you while you're in the hospital.

By definition, a hospitalist is a doctor or advanced practice clinician whose entire medical practice is dedicated to caring for admitted patients inside a hospital. They take care of you from the point that you are admitted until you are discharged. They get to know you in order to provide optimum care. Once you are discharged from the hospital, you are returned back to your primary care practitioner. Hospitalists have to do an excellent job of making sure your medical records are correct and up to date. The handoff has to include those excellent notes, so the PCP can pick your care up where it was left off.

Tip #13 Just learning.....Students!

Many medical facilities allow students from all types of medical professions to participate in patient care. You may interact with all types of students - medical, respiratory, physical and occupational therapy, physician assistant, advanced practice nursing, nursing, phlebotomy, on and on. When asked if it's ok to have a student present, please agree to do so! Your condition and/or treatment plan could be unique, something they have not ever come across as part of their studies. Why wouldn't you want to have another set of eyes and ears to listen to your story? Again the answer is: **YOU DON'T!** They can do a great job of taking your medical history, since they won't want to leave any detail out. They really have no idea how many questions their supervisor may have for them; the care is in the minutia they gather!

Tip #14 Don't underestimate who is scrubbing the floors of your hospital room!

Environmental services workers (EVS), otherwise known as custodians, can be great messengers of issues you need addressed. For instance, if the nursing staff is running behind in administering your pain medications, the EVS employee can inform the nurses of how much pain you are in. Most EVS staff will listen to patients' woes. They also have alerted the nursing staff many times about the patients who may have face-planted.

Be glad there's another set of ears who can listen to any woes you may have and help be a messenger as part of your health care team.

Tip #15 Nursing or physician supervisors, yep they are in charge!

Do you ever wonder if there is a person in charge to contact within the medical facility where you get care? The obvious answer is YES there is! There is always someone in the chain of command who can listen to your issues, don't ever be told otherwise! General staff may not know exactly who is in charge, but a simple call to the hospital switchboard can help you to figure out who that one person may be that can answer your questions. If you are on the hospital floor and things don't seem quite right, there is always a nursing supervisor. Many "teaching" hospitals designate an attending physician to be in charge!

Believe it or not, higher level administrative staff are 'on call' on a regular basis.

Of course, most days we have no idea of who is in charge, as part of the business hierarchy. Just know that someone IS in charge. Since healthcare is run as a business model, most healthcare executives don't want negativity regarding the care their employees are producing as a whole.

The same mindset goes for outpatient medical clinics, there is always a practice manager or operations manager associated with these. Of course, they are on one of the rungs of the company hierarchy if the outpatient office is part of a larger healthcare system. If by any chance, it is an 'independent' practice, you can ask for the 'office or practice' manager.

What you don't want to happen is to have an issue and not get a resolution to the issue. The longer it goes, the bigger the issue gets. Time is of the essence always! By registering your dissatisfaction with what is happening, you at least know that you have been heard. Medical practices tend to want to insure you are happy with the services they provide.

Appointments

Tip #16 APPOINTMENTS, *APPOINTMENTS*, Appointments......?? Urgent!

As most folks know sometimes it is very difficult to get into their medical provider in what would seem to be a reasonable amount of time. Six months generally isn't considered a timely basis! Before you hang up the phone with the scheduler, ask to be placed on a cancelation list or on what some systems call, "fast pass". Also ask the scheduler to look at the overall schedule and ask them to see if there might be some unassigned appointments that could be gotten. Often times, the providers have no idea how difficult it is to get in to be seen by them. I have heard from providers that they ask their practice managers and/or schedulers to open up as many appointments as possible. If you follow some of these steps, you may go from a six month wait to a much shorter time.

A large reminder is that if you don't get a quicker time, **call back everyday!** There are always cancellations on any given day. The day you may call could be your lucky day!

As a side note, if you need to get in to see a **specialist**, have your primary care provider, add the word **URGENT** across the top to the referral they are sending. This can cut the wait time down by a lot! Truly, if you need to see a specialist, there is a very good reason for that referral. I wouldn't believe that your PCP would want you to wait months to get in, especially if there is a possibility of an undiagnosed cancer!

I never believe that health care should be based on luck, only on need.

Tip #17 ? ? ? Carry the list with you.....remember there are NO stupid questions!

There are no stupid questions in health care. NOT A ONE! No matter who the medical provider is, there's NO STUPID QUESTION!

Do yourself a favor and make a list of questions that YOU

need answers to! This will not only cut down on time, but it will also keep you from forgetting a really really important question. You know how it goes, you get home and wish you had asked something! And if you are facing a difficult medical journey, the list will help you to get the answers you need.

As part of the question asking process, never assume there aren't alternatives to what is being suggested for treatment. Be diligent and direct with your questions. If the answers head you down a path where there doesn't seem to be much they can do or they simply can't or won't do, be adamant. Be persistent with your asks.

If someone can go with you to your appointment, please take them! Two sets of ears, two sets of eyes are better than one, especially if you are anxious about the treatment path. Many of us have our eyes glaze over as we listen, for example, to the surgeon describe what he or she will be doing to our body. It's human nature! Your mind will be put at ease, if the other person can write while you listen!

*my notes:*____

____

Tip #18 "We never got the request!"

Have you ever called your provider's office to request an appointment, explaining to the person on the other end of the phone that your primary care provider sent a fax, only to have the person on the other end tell you, "No, we haven't received a request yet!" Sometimes a primary care office may fax multiple times, but still nothing shows up! Although, you would think there would be a dedicated person 'taking off the faxes' one by one and getting the person's medical issues reviewed in order to give an appointment—that is no longer the case. With the advent of modern technology, the referrals or requests land in a computer based system where they may be reviewed in some kind of order. I once had to ask my primary care provider to fax no less than four times for a diagnostic study appointment. Finally, I asked to have the request faxed to me and I sent it through. Fortunately, the person on the other end of the phone was cordial enough to watch for my fax. Voila, the fax arrived, the test was scheduled same day! It's often about having perseverance and not taking "no" for an answer!

Tip #19 The money guard, how the front desk person collects the money.

Believe it or not, healthcare systems around the country are always looking for ways to collect the money owed them by their patients. It is understandable they have the obligation to collect the money. They need cash in order to keep the lights on, the employees paid, and the equipment up to date. However, it's how the question gets asked and by whom, that makes this a sensitive topic.

One of the best and often times humiliating ways they collect the balance is to have the person that checks you in for your appointment to ask, "Would you want to pay your bill today?". A lot of times there are other people within ear shot, who not only hear the amount, but who also hear your response. I don't care how much your balance is, $10 or $10,000, this is NOT the time to ask. Can you spell embarrassment?

Before you whip out your credit or debit card, checkbook,

or cash from your wallet, quietly tell the person, "I will deal with this at another time, not here and now!" This is an excellent statement, since there just might be 'discount offers' to be made with the actual billing office. If you pay the bill in full at the moment of humiliation, you may run the risk of missing out on these 'discounts'. **Reminder: you are the patient in all things, both in your care and in your finances!**

The person at the front desk may be mortified they even are asking the question, but it is simply written into their job description to do so. As part of their requirement to ask, they should be schooled on compassion and understanding as well!

I have no idea if there are any bonuses or prizes offered for the most money collected in a day. If that possibility exists, then it becomes understandable why some act like bullies! **DON'T LET THEM BULLY YOU! Ask for a supervisor to address the issue.**

Always always always do all of this with kindness, keep your cool!

Remember billing is billing and appointments are appointments.

Tip #20 On hold, then push #1, option #3! A pet peeve that can be improved upon!

Have you ever dialed for an appointment and been given five or six options to listen to and then forget what the number of the option is that you are supposed to select? It happens a lot. If I had a dime for every time I have had to go back and listen to the whole menu, I could have retired long ago! Seriously, you feel sick as a dog or you are on your 'break' with limited time, then you are subjected to a phone menu. Some systems will hang up on you if you don't choose, rather than transferring your call to an 'operator'. I often wonder why they add yet another layer of difficulty to improving your health.

Have you ever wanted to make an appointment and have to listen to "Fly Me to the Moon" for ten to fifteen minutes after you have hit #1, then option #3? I know that medical facilities want to cut corners on costs, but it would go a long way to have a live person answer the phone and forward the call. Often times, once you have a live person on the phone, they can facilitate where the call needs to be directed and a whole lot quicker!

I always say my time is valuable like everyone else's, but medical facilities have no knowledge of what that means. For instance, if I start at caller #5 in the queue and advance down to caller #1, meaning that I should have the ability to now talk to someone, but only to wait another ten minutes. There is something wrong with that logic, either on my part or on the automated system's part.

This is a note to those CEOs who may be reading this, can we please improve this process, PLEASE?!?

Tip #21 After visit summaries, what are they and why are they important?

You have an appointment and when you are checking out, the person at the desk asks if you want your after-visit summary (AVS). You may not want to have a stack of papers to carry with you, but it can be wise to take them. Once you have them, you can put them in the folder you started for these specific documents. If you don't like the thought of killing trees and having pieces of paper, you should always double check to see that they are indeed in your patient portal. A lot of electronic medical records now can display the actual note your medical provider has written. The AVS can also contain important instructions and appointments that you medical provider have given. It's important to check the AVS to make sure your medication and allergy lists are correct. Remember when the nurse or nursing assistant was asking you about your medications and allergies, they then will show up on the AVS. In the event they may have clicked on something by mistake, it is a good idea to verify on that AVS what now has been updated in the system. Review of your medical records is good on many levels as has been discussed before.

Tip #22 Survey says.......ARE THEY WORTH COMPLETING?

We all have been the recipients of a famous patient survey from Press-Ganey. Many healthcare systems across the country utilize surveys to determine how well things are going at their institutions. The survey link is sent almost immediately to your cell phone or email after you have been evaluated and treated by your medical provider. Be aware the surveys are not a free service for the healthcare institution; they pay for the use of them and the generation of the data analysis. Some healthcare systems base any bonus pays to the medical providers on the outcome of these surveys. Oh, you didn't know that medical providers are rewarded for their performance, well you do now! There are many elements of care associated with corresponding bonuses. If you are interested, you can use a search engine to get a better understanding of healthcare bonuses.

The surveys don't need to be just about submitting complaints for any care received, but they can also transmit the kudos for the stellar parts of the care received.

There are usually places on the surveys, where you can type or write a response. I encourage folks to write their joys or their unhappiness in those places. YES, YES, YES, the comments are actually read and collated by someone in the administration office of the healthcare facility/system. Never relay your thoughts or comments anonymously; you believe what you believe and know. Have the courage and conviction of the comments to leave your phone number and/or email address! Don't be surprised when you either receive a phone call or an email from someone asking to talk about what your thoughts are regarding your care.

Business of Healthcare

Tip #23 Collections....now what! The elephant in the room!

You thought by not opening and looking at the medical bills, they would magically disappear. Unfortunately, in this country, healthcare is a business. Being a business means services rendered requires a payment of some kind, either through insurance or via your own wallet.

Usually, there are four billing cycles before you are sent to collections. Collections companies make money by collecting your owed debt. There is no better incentive for the powers that be in these companies, to know your profitability relies on collecting that debt. They usually seem heartless, but realizing their motivation explains their behavior.

The last thing you need in your life while you are sick is to have to endure the non-stop phone calls, emails, and/or text messages. **Never ignore the phone calls, emails, and/or text messages; talk to someone!** They will just become more relentless as time goes on. Address the elephant in the room and get it some peanuts—explain the situation you are in, what you can potentially pay, and ask them to document your comments.

Avoid the elephant in the room— saying it loudly for those in the back of the room who hasn't heard this before!!

The key is to open the medical bill and address it post haste. The person on the end of the line at the billing office can note in their computer that you have called. **Please please please explain how ill you may still be and that once you are somewhat back on your feet, you would be happy to talk about the bill.** In the event, you get an immovable force on the other end, you can offer to pay something. While you are chatting, ask for any patient discounts that are available. If this medical issue has caused you to work less hours and have decreased income, ask about the ability to get help with the bill. Whether that help is in the form of a financial assistance application or to potentially apply for Medicaid, you **HAVE** to ask!

You can also ask that you not be sent to collections as you navigate your illness or recovery.

It's always about a good faith effort on your part.

Tip #24 ASK THIS QUESTION!

As patients, we often ask healthcare facilities "do you take my insurance?" By all means, please ask that question, but add to it, "are you in my insurance network?"

A lot of frontline staff have no idea what kind of insurance is taken by their practice or their healthcare system and if you are in network or out of network. Health insurance contracts are added and removed on a regular basis, meaning it's difficult to keep up! By asking the above questions, you can avoid some unintended consequences. Two that specifically come to mind:

1. Having to pay higher amounts of out-of-pocket dollars and/or if not all of the bill
2. Navigating an appeals process that can become quite time consuming

Keep in mind, the best person to ask those questions of are the billing people of the medical facility. Better yet, take the time to ask your insurance company—if they don't know, then nobody knows!

Tip #25 Don't forget about prior authorizations!

Lets talk about prior authorizations. Usually the medical provider's staff submits a 'prior auth' request to the insurance company. This can be for all kinds of things, medications, equipment, diagnostic testing, etc. The request is filled out and someone in the health insurance world reviews the request and it's either approved or denied. The medical provider can submit alternatives to what they originally asked for to get an approval. A lot of times for medications, the answer will be you have to try another medication before they will pay for the next generation or the more expensive one. This is where excellent documentation comes into play—supporting medical documentation is usually a vital key to getting things approved!

Tip #26 KNOW THY BENEFITS!

It is imperative to learn and know what your actual insurance benefits are—it doesn't matter if you have (a) commercial [mostly employer sponsored coverage], (b) Medicaid, or (c) Medicare.

The fastest way to find the contact info for those benefits is to look on the back of your insurance card. When you do call, you will hear a repeated message over and over about accessing the insurance company's portal. Although this may be easier for the health insurance company's call center, to avoid fielding questions over the phone, it doesn't always help to get the answers you may need on a more timely basis. The response of your questions via the portal, whether it is by engaging in a "chat" option, should allow you to print the transcript of that "chat", or once the response is sent to your email, that would become your documentation. Remember that any documentation lays the knowledge groundwork for the path ahead, especially if you have to dispute what may have been said or written! Knowledge really is power - and self-defense.

REMINDER: Most phone calls are 'recorded' for quality assurance' purposes. If push comes to shove, you can always ask for them to review their transcripts to ascertain what was said on the phone call.

When engaging with others on the phone, **always, always, always be kind**, even if your head feels like it is going to explode at any moment! Keep your cool!

If you don't like or don't understand the information you are being given, ask for a SUPERVISOR!

Tip #27 Never assume your provider understands

your health insurance coverage.

Most medical providers can only guess at what your health insurance covers. Some electronic medical records can help them especially with medication coverage. Many times they will order a test, a medication, a piece of equipment with hope in their face that what they are ordering will be covered. They have no idea if your deductible has been met or what your co-insurance looks like. Their standard answer and/or question is "I am not sure if this is covered, maybe you might?!"

Sadly, this means they may have to order something different after you have discovered your insurance won't cover or only covers partially what's being ordered. I say sadly because that means you have to go down a rabbit hole with them in tow. It means sending either a portal message or making a phone call. This costs you time and costs them time. To some extent, if the order is sent to the pharmacy or the medical equipment company, it costs the pharmacy time, and costs the medical equipment provider time since they may the ordered prescription or order the medical equipment. Unless you can get your insurance company on the phone during the appointment to find out exactly how things are covered, you are started down a rabbit hole.

There is no sage advice other than navigating the rabbit hole you are in. Hopefully one day, we'll do better with this particular issue.

Tip #28 Uncompensated care known by another name, "charity care"!

Many Americans suffer sticker shock when they receive hospital medical bills. If they are the uninsured, the big question is, "How am I ever going to be able to pay this?" Of course, being sick and having to worry about the medical bill is double whammy. The thoughts of the medical bill can seriously impede recovery.

Most hospital systems have some sort of uncompensated care (UC) or 'charity care' funds in place. If after you have applied for Medicaid and have been denied, you could apply for the uncompensated care funding. In order to receive any type of funding, you have to complete a 'financial assistance' application. In addition to the application itself, you are asked for pertinent financial information. Although it may seem like yet another hoop to have to jump through, it can be worth the attempt. Some hospital systems once they approve the UC can then provide at least six months of care to the patient, without the fear of getting medical bills.

A lot of folks don't take advantage of this because they have no idea such a thing exists. Rather than throwing the bill into a pile waiting for collections to hit, contact the hospital system to see what the possibilities are. It may well be worth the phone call!

Tip #29 Deny, deny....Appeal, appeal! Don't forget about prior authorizations!

We have all had this happen at one time or another, a denial by the insurance company for a procedure the medical provider has deemed as necessary. All of the boxes have been checked as to why it is medically necessary. But somewhere in the health insurance world, a denial is issued. The denial may come back with other alternative therapies that are needed before they will **Approve** the diagnostic testing or procedure is completed.

Always ALWAYS *ALWAYS* challenge the denial. Most likely they don't have all of the pertinent information. Always involve your medical provider and their staff in the denial process. Believe me this won't be their first rodeo. Over the course of their careers, they probably have written hundreds of letters to support why the insurance company should approve the requests.

If the medical provider has an opportunity, they can speak with the medical provider at the insurance company. They can talk oranges to oranges instead of apples to oranges, meaning they know and understand the medical jargon to get their point across!

If you have the ability to have a three-way conversation with the medical provider staff and the insurance company at the same time, **DO IT**! This way everyone hears the same thing at the same time. Of course, take very detailed notes.

More likely than not, you can get the denial overturned. The statistics are glaring for how many get overturned, for some treatments, 7 out of 10 get overturned. But it takes grit and perseverance to make it happen.

Tip #30 Review Your Medical Billing!

Many of us have the "deer caught in the headlight" look when it comes to medical billing. There are numbers and letters with little explanation of what any of that means. Ironically, your medical services are captured and put into a nice neat document called an 'EOB' or an explanation of benefits. Most of us can decipher parts of it and we can usually get to the 'bottom line' of what we may really owe or not really owe. I believe medical billing and medical insurance determinations are like the Wizard of Oz - nobody not even the bean counters of either the healthcare systems or the health insurance companies truly understand what it all means—they just know that they have been handed spreadsheet after spreadsheet and told to keep expanding them. The spreadsheets are the obvious driver of what we know as healthcare, the business model.

If you have ever looked at what is billed by a healthcare facility or practice and then look at what is paid, rarely is the 'billed' the same as 'paid'. Enter the CONTRACT! What most folks don't realize is that there is a contract that occurs between the health care provider and the health insurance company. Which means that many times no matter how smart you think you are, you can't understand something that is almost not fully understood by even the smartest of minds without knowing their contract requirements.

Medical bills are generated shortly after services are rendered. I caution folks not to immediately write a check for the balance owed. It is extremely important to make sure what is billed is WHAT YOU actually OWE. Sometimes, the coding is incorrect and the insurance company hasn't weighed in on what they are actually paying. If you have ever had to ask for a refund from a healthcare system/provider, it sometimes can take an act of God to get that to happen. If you think there will be an immediate refund of your funds that you paid in, a lot of larger facilities do an 'audit' or sweep of accounts, but that happens according to their rules, and is not dependent upon the fact the money would be great in your pocket, especially if it means being able to buy groceries or medications.

Safety

Tip #31 Infection rate, WHAT?!

If you are scheduled to see any type of specialist for a surgical procedure, you **need to ask what their infection rate is for the procedure you're having done**. This question is important for any joint replacements. An orthopedic surgeon can share their infection rate, believe it or not, they take pride in a 0% or as close to that as possible. Surgeons of any type are dedicated to their craft and never relish having a patient getting infected.

In today's world there are 2 types of surgery facilities; in-hospital or an ambulatory surgery center. You can find the infection rates for both types of facilities. It's probably easier to obtain the infection rate from the ambulatory surgery center, since they are typically smaller and are traditionally designed to do one or two types of surgery.

Hospital surgical suites can do many types of surgeries, from gall bladder removals to brain surgery. Some hospitals have designated operating rooms for each type of surgery they do. This can cut down on the rate of infections. Any infection gotten from a hospital procedure is known as a *nosocomial infection*. There are lots of reasons for nosocomial infections, including believe it or not, something as simple as poor handwashing techniques.

Any time a cut is made into a body part, there is a risk of the patient developing an infection. Infections cost the healthcare systems a lot of money to get the patient well again. With that understanding, there is a large investment into making sure that infection rates are at a low level.

Most people are aware of "Google" reviews. Reviews are everywhere, from how good a mechanic at a garage was, at fixing your car to how good the service was at your local restaurant. Health care is no different in generating reviews. And as usual, we have to keep in mind that anyone can leave a review and say anything they would like, good or bad. When it comes to health care, people may bear their soul as to their experiences so no other patient has to endure mediocre care. Not all reviews are in the negative; believe it or not, patients love to tout the expertise of their medical provider. Read reviews and analyze what is being written. You will need to decide if you think they are a valid reflection of your medical provider. If your gut tells you to run and run very quickly, you may want to do just that.

Tip #32 Have a complaint, there's a Board for that!

Not often do folks need to think about complaints. But sometimes, events and issues happen to make you want to file a complaint because there's no resolution. You try and try to make the entities understand what you're trying to say to no avail. There are all types of boards that license the medical professionals you may come in contact with as you receive healthcare. Typically the members of these boards are appointed by the Governor and confirmed by the Senate. Examples include the State Board of Medicine, State Board of Osteopathic Medicine, State Board of Nursing, State Board of Insurance, Pharmacy Board, Department of Human Services, etc. You can submit complaints and then their investigators investigate the complaints. If there is merit to the complaint, the investigators can then forward the complaints to the prosecutors for the state. The prosecutors then decide if a disciplinary action is warranted. Facility complaints travel a similar path.

Valid complaints and their resolutions can be helpful to healthcare. Frivolous or baseless complaints can bog down the system, which means getting the important fixes for things like better nursing home care.

Tip #33 How safe is safe?

Most hospital systems have in place risk management, as well as safety committees. As you can only imagine, there's a lot of patient care taking place within the walls of a hospital and any outpatient auxiliary buildings.

Staff are busy and they are human. Sometimes a simple ask by you or your loved one, "what medication is that"; "what's in the IV"; "why's the lab-work needed", "could I be allergic to that", or "why are you marking that knee" etc. can put your mind at ease when it comes to your care. I haven't known anyone who doesn't have a small amount of angst when it comes to being a patient.

Why do I bring this topic up: because medication errors, wrong site surgeries, allergic reactions, etc. happen on a daily basis. Hospital systems review a lot of these types of things. They also analyze the "near misses", in other words, something that could have had a detrimental effect on your care, had someone not double or triple checked.

Bottom line is you should always ask what someone is about to do you and if they get offended, so be it! Healthcare professionals are human just like you! The one question you ask could save your life or the life of your loved one!

Tip #34 Starting a new medication?

We all have been ordered a new medication. The medical provider makes an assumption there won't be any issues; they write for a 90-day supply. You go to the pharmacy to pick up the medication, bring it home, and take one dose. It doesn't take long until you are experiencing an allergic reaction. Now you have 89 or more doses left.

I would suggest that when you are getting the prescription filled, ask for only a few pills. This means that if there are any issues, you won't have to discard the entire amount of the prescription. Can you ask to do this? YES! It may mean a few more steps for pharmacist, but it will help your purse strings. And depending on what the medication is, such as a narcotic—you won't want them just lying around the house.

Tip #35 What's the real instructions? To fast or not to fast?

We have all been sent to have diagnostic labs drawn. But do we always get - and more importantly understand - the instructions? For every lab test you may be sent for, it is imperative to make sure you have all the information needed to produce the most optimum of results. By ensuring that you have the correct instructions, it will save you any repeat labs or being sent down a treatment rabbit hole that isn't necessary.

For instance, you are sent for labs and you didn't realize you needed to fast for at least eight hours. Right before you have the labs done, you eat a large breakfast. Once you get the lab results back, there are multiple things elevated. The medical provider looks at the results and at first glance may decide the elevated values need to be treated. Hopefully before any treatment would get initiated, you would be able to admit you did eat right before the labs were drawn. Hopefully any values would be compared to previous labs if they exist.

Do yourself a favor, ALWAYS ALWAYS ask, if there are any **SPECIAL INSTRUCTIONS!** Your arm, wallet, and medical provider will be glad you did!

Tip #36 Crickets, what happens when nobody calls you with the results?

Have you ever had your diagnostic test results land in your patient portal shortly after your test? Sometimes the results are good and sometimes not so good! There are 'highs' and 'lows' spotlighted.

You look at the results range and think, "Should I be worried?" about that number or that result on an x-ray? Since most of us don't have certifications or degrees, I would say let it up to those that do.

But what happens when you just don't hear about the results? It's now 48 hours later and crickets - no phone call or portal message. The best idea is **NOT** to wait for them to call, but rather pick up the phone and **CALL THEM**. You can send a message on the portal, again a simple one, no "War and Peace" needed:

"Hi, I saw my tests were back! Could you let me know the results, please?"

As **patients** we **NEED** to take the **initiative**. If that means when we haven't heard from anyone, calling or emailing them should be **OUR** next step. Gone are the days where medical practices are slow; many now have to turn patients away. Understanding that can go a long way for better care. I know, I know - I long for the old days when medical providers reached out on a regular basis. Believe it or not at the free medical clinic I founded, every patient was called after their visit to make sure they understood what happened at the visit and to double check if there was anything needed. That my fellow patients is UTOPIA!

I will tell you that if you have a 'critical' report, they will call and call until they can get in touch with you! Critical reports can be a matter of life and death. Most medical facilities and providers already know this. They know that if a critical value hits their desk, they need to be speaking with you and what the possible next steps are pretty darn quickly.

Understanding critical lab values are high on the triage list, means not letting the medical provider off the hook because your labs are not critical. There needs to be a communication loop completed. Believe it or not, some providers' staff will call you even if your labs are within normal limits (WNL). It gives them the opportunity to ask you how you are feeling and if you have any questions!

Tip #37 Make Sure Lab Specimens Are Labeled Correctly.

When was the last time that a phlebotomy technician showed you they were putting the correct label, with your name and date of birth on it?

A lot of times, the phlebotomy technician simply collects the sample and puts the printed label on the collection tube and you have no idea if that is actually your label and your specimen, since the tech could have printed out the wrong label. Does it happen often, maybe not or maybe it does, only the safety committee of your hospital knows the answer to that! But to avoid being stuck for a second time because there was a mistake made with your blood - be proactive and ASK TO SEE THE LABEL on your sample!

Tip #38 Getting discharged, do you really have what you need?

Yay, you are getting discharged. Here's a subtle reminder to try to be focused as you're being discharged. If you ever have been discharged from a hospital stay or an outpatient procedure, you know the drill. You get dressed! The nursing staff comes in to provide you with discharge paperwork and will expect you or someone to sign off on what they are speed reading at times. There are lots of assumptions that you may really understand what's being said. However, you may have just had anesthesia, which can cloud your thinking or you are just beyond excited to being sprung.

Make sure you ask if your prescriptions have been sent in and to where - there is nothing pleasant about needing pain medications, when your pain level is over the top and finding out the prescription didn't make it to the pharmacy. Pharmacies usually aren't open 24 hours, which means you could go a long time without your pain medications! UGH!

Along those same lines, if you are being discharged later in the day and you know that your pharmacy will close before you can get there, ask for a few pills to get your through until your pharmacy opens the next day. Hopefully, whoever may be discharging you would actually suggest the possibility.

You need medical equipment that was thought to be ordered, but you find out it will be another 24 hours before it is delivered. Hobbling around is dangerous! A hospital bed can be a godsend, as you are struck trying to get out of your own bed.

Home health and outpatient therapy services can be helpful, but sometimes the orders get sent to the incorrect place or they can't be scheduled in a timely manner. Yep, a delay in being evaluated and getting the services started sooner than later does not bode well for continued healing and recovery.

Questions asked before you leave the confines of the building and getting the best answers will save an immense amount of frustration for you and for any caregiver you may have.

Ask, clarify, ask, clarify those instructions, UNTIL YOU UNDERSTAND!

Patient Care

Tip #39 Not Recovering Like The Statistics Say...

Every patient is an individual. So, whatever procedure you are having done or the illness you have, remember that you are unique. In other words, we all heal and recover at a different pace. Never compare yourself to your neighbor or family member! The neighbor or family member could be much healthier, takes no medications, works out every day. To compare yourself equally, you would have to be the same in every facet. If you aren't, then compare yourself to the beginning of the recovery journey to where you may be at any given moment. Remind yourself, you have come a long way, baby!

For example, an orthopedic surgeon may tell you after your knee replacement, all should be good in six – eight weeks. They arrive at this statement, by understanding the best case scenario and the worst case scenario. If at eight weeks and beyond, you are still having difficulty, yes it could be worth a call to their office.

In the utopian medical world where all patients are created equal and they follow instructions to the nth degree, then yes, it is possible that at the mentioned mark, you should be right as rain. But again, we are all humans, some of us follow directions to the letter and others do not.

Remember you know your body the best! If something doesn't feel right, call, communicate your issues to someone in the office! Don't ever feel like you are a bother! Better to call than to look back and have the would-have, should-have syndrome!

Tip #40 When in doubt, get it checked out!

We all have a tendency to be in denial when it comes to medical issues. "It hurts, but it doesn't hurt that much!" "My chest feels funny, but it must have been something I ate!" We come up with lots of excuses as to why we shouldn't seek care. The unknown is scary, it really is! "What if I go and it's something really bad?" runs through a lot of our minds. But what if going to seek treatment would stop you from becoming sicker? Like there are no stupid questions, there are also no stupid reasons for seeking health care, including having no healthcare coverage.

GO!

Be aware, if you have no healthcare coverage, there is help out there to help with the billing. Don't avoid seeking care because you are so afraid of the bill! Dying should never be the only option.

I will say this again very loudly, when in doubt, get whatever is ailing you checked out! Don't wait!

Shop Around

Tip #41 Shop around for a better price; yep, there are less expensive diagnostic tests.

You are given an order for either an MRI or a CT scan. Before you schedule, do yourself a favor and shop around for the best price. Include using your insurance or simply paying cash for the tests in your research. Obviously this is for non-emergent testing where timing is not of the essence. If there are competing healthcare systems, you can check the prices. If there are outpatient radiology groups, you can check the prices.

Of course, you have to know what your insurance particulars are. Don't shop unless you know your deductible and any co-insurances. Once you have all of the information, then you can compare apples to apples and oranges to oranges.

Checking a 'cash' price for any of these tests is wise. If you pay cash, you can save hundreds of dollars. But again, compare 'out of pocket' costs using your insurance to just paying cash.

Tip #42 COMPARE Prescription prices—There's an app for that!

Just because you have healthcare coverage, doesn't mean you have to use it for your prescriptions. If you do a comparison, you may end up saving money by simply paying cash and not using your medical insurance card. There are multiple prescription help programs out there, things like *GoodRx* [https://www.goodrx.com], and *NeedyMeds* [https://www.needymeds.org]. *GoodRx* lists your prescription medications, along with the cash pricing and where you can get the prescription at a much better price. *NeedyMeds* is an advocacy group that can help with prescription assistance programs and drug discount cards, where you can get the prescription at a better price.

If you have no coverage at all, most pharmaceutical companies offer prescription assistance programs (PAP). A simple application could if approved snag you a year's worth of medications. These are great for those on insulin or on higher priced respiratory inhalers.

ADVOCATE STORIES

These are actual experiences I and my client patients have encountered in my years as an advocate. Each has a lesson for you to do better when it happens to someone you love.

There's a button for that!

A seventy-eight year old patient Harold was having problems with their prostate. The recommendation by his urologist was to insert an artificial urethral implant to help with the urine flow.

The procedure happened in December. Healing had to occur in that the body was actually accepting this device. Two months later in February, the surgeon decided that it was time to actually activate the device. Initially the device worked, urine flowed well.

Two weeks into the activation, the patient started to have small to large clots in his urine. The worst part was that he had to set an alarm for every 45 minutes in order to wake up to urinate. This went on for another week. The surgeon's office was called, appointment scheduled. The patient was unable to meet with the surgeon but instead had to meet with one of his residents. The patient voiced his concerns, the response from the resident was, "We don't really know how to help you!" The patient having done their own research had asked about hyperbaric oxygen (HBO) treatments. All of a sudden, he was getting a referral to another facility to start hyperbaric oxygen (HBO) treatments. The medical provider, the nurse, and the tech at the HBO office had placed several calls with messages to talk about the patient due to the concerns they had about the treatments they were providing to the patient. None of the messages were returned. Both the patient and the HBO medical team were frustrated—the HBO team knew that the patient was suffering and something was incorrect.

The family reached out with the caveat they didn't want to bother me for help. With the behind-the-scenes connections I had, I emailed explaining the situation and the patient needed help. The patient then received a phone call from the head of the urology department, but unfortunately, he had to leave a message. Phone tag ensued. The patient never did end up meeting with the head of the department.

Finally, the patient had had enough with the bleeding and the sleep deprivation. He decided to go to the ER. We spoke and I had given him explicit instructions to call ahead to the urology doctor on call and explain that he was headed there, otherwise he would have had to sit in the ER waiting area for more hours with the back-up of urine continuing, along with the discomfort. He did just that, got a resident on the phone who came off as rude to him. The phone call did afford him the opportunity to be taken to another area to wait. The same resident who had spoken with him on the phone came out of surgery to meet with him. In a matter of only five 5 minutes he found out that he actually had the ability to press a button to de-activate the implant on his own, so that urine could flow freely if needed to.

As the resident's fellow co-workers, including the surgeon, were throwing up their hands in defeat, the resident provided the simplest solution to improve his quality of life.

There are several missteps in this patient's care and valuable lessons to be learned. The patient himself could not get his medical team to understand how truly awful he felt, despite the multiple messages left for them. One of them thought he had an entirely different device inserted! Communication and connection were lacking among all of the healthcare folks. Who actually knows whether the patient was provided adequate instructions or the simple solution was left out of any of those instructions.

Why did he wait?

I encountered Bernie in the free medical clinic for the working insured I had founded. Bernie, who was 42, had come to the clinic because his mother, a nurse had coaxed him to do so. His complaints were pretty significant. He was having problems eating and keeping things down. Bernie, a magnificent craftsman, had had no health insurance. In completing our intake form, he indicated on the form he was uninsured because he was not a fan of President Obama. Of course, President Obama brought to fruition the Affordable Care Act, otherwise known as Obamacare. Having answered the question very truthfully, he was very upfront. I on the other hand was in disbelief someone would actually allow a political belief get in the way of their potential care. He could have had health insurance, at probably a very reasonable price.

He arrived in the clinic looking very ashen and washed out. Of course who wouldn't be if they had been only able to eat minimally for days, right?! He was examined and evaluated. It was highly recommended that he go to the emergency room to have at the very least some lab-work drawn and a possible CT scan of his abdomen. Feeling awful and having his mother at his side, he agreed. We sent them off with all of our medical notes to be hand carried to the emergency room.

Early the next morning, when we were able to review the emergency room findings, my heart sunk. He did indeed have masses on both his pancreas and his liver. The phone rang in the clinic only a short time later. Bernie's mother was on the other end of the line sobbing quietly.

Bernie, after getting the results of the CT scan and the labs, had decided he wanted no further treatment. His mother being a nurse knew full well what that would mean for her only son's existence on this planet - it was going to be cut short by the cancer that had been growing inside of him. Since he wanted hospice care right away, the arrangements were made. This all happened on a Friday. By the end of the day, everything was in place for Bernie to begin the road to death. Full disclosure here, after leaving the clinic that day, there was no way to stop the tears rolling down my face. All I could think was, here was a very talented craftsman, whose life was ending way too soon because he refused to accept insurance coverage brought about by a black President of the United States. It was a senseless way to die.

He made it through the weekend, with some rough patches, but he made it. But suddenly those rough patches turned into tumultuous times with lots of pain and agony. On Tuesday, his mom called the clinic to let me know, that he had passed away after having vomited a lot of blood. She held the son she had given birth to in her arms as he took his last breath.

I could only imagine the pain she and his dad endured watching all of this unfold. There was no way to go backwards to fix any of it. Bernie was gone and along with him went many many potential creative projects that would not be created. The world has missed out on his many talents!

Foreign Care!

I have met and heard of patients seeking care outside of the United States. I have also met patients from other countries who have come here to visit and have needed health care while here.

An acquaintance who was moving to another country but who was also having medical issues prior to the move was anxious about the care where they were moving to. They had a long talk with their medical provider about postponing the move and getting the procedure done here in the states. The medical provider's advice was to move forward with the move. They advised the country they were moving to would provide them with excellent care and quite possibly better than what they might receive here.

Another acquaintance has a wife born in one of the European countries, entitling her to universal health care. While there, the husband planned to have his lab-work done. The timing right for the usually scheduled lab work to be drawn. He understood the country to have a great health care system. On his arrival, the doctors informed him that because he was not a citizen of the country, they would sadly be required to bill him for the service – all of $50 American dollars. The same lab work would have cost at least $200 dollars here in the states. It always amazes me, comparing the costs vs anywhere else in the world, and the glaring difference. He also is in need of an MRI, $500 here vs much less there. Due to companies having the ability to sell globally, there is no difference in the equipment used here or there.

Another acquaintance explained to me how the United States differs in comparison to their own country. They had a major life-threatening event and needed life-saving care. They told me about the cost of their procedures which were only one tenth of the cost of what it would have been here in the US. $15,000 there vs $150,000 here. Every person in their country receives full coverage from birth until they turn eighteen. After that, every adult pays a monthly amount and once they reach an annual amount of only a few hundred dollars, they receive care for free. Their outcomes are better than here in the United States. Shockingly, the health insurance companies there pay into a fund for those who may not be able to afford the monthly payments or the annual payments. They literally ensure everyone gets the health care they deserve and need.

Sleepless nights worrying about the outstanding medical bill!

Mark had received all of the approvals for a cardiac treatment which would save his heart by bringing it back into normal rhythm. The insurance company put in writing he was 'prior authed' for his procedure. He proceeded to have it done. Weeks later he started receiving medical bills in excess of $100,000. He was astounded and confused. Then started the sleepless nights worrying about how he was going to pay the bill. Multiple phone calls to both the health insurance company and the healthcare system produced no results. Ironically, I had just started offering classes on how to play the healthcare game. He showed up with his story of what had happened and how his health was being affected.

After a three-way phone call with the healthcare system and then the health insurance company, along with multiple emails—it was determined there had been a mistake in the billing and the submission. In other words, neither entity was accepting the blame for their mistakes. He finally could sleep knowing that neither his credit score wasn't going to be affected and that he wasn't on the hoof for the $100K+. I could hear in his voice the absolute relief!

Yanking of their healthcare!

Josh and Karen, a husband and wife, was terminated their Medicaid after years of being on it. Karen, who had just spent over 4 months in the hospital and was recovering was told their Medicaid had been terminated at the end of the month. Josh is a diabetic and is on a GLP-1 would now need to spend in excess of $900 in order to keep his sugars under control. Karen continued to fill up with fluid after being discharged and was still in dire need of follow up care. Besides the present healthcare issues she was dealing with she also had to stop her breast cancer medications. Those medications were prescribed for prevention of the breast cancer reoccurring.

Nothing had changed with their Medicaid renewal. They had done everything that was asked of them, submitting all of the needed documentation. In fact, they not only submitted it once, but multiple times. Not sure we will ever know where all of the copies of their documents went, which black hole or vat they landed in.

They were mailed letters about the termination of their Medicaid, along with a letter alerting them to apply for health insurance through the Affordable Care Act Exchange. The reason they ended up on Medicaid was they couldn't afford the health insurance premium of $600. It was then discovered they would definitely qualify for Medicaid due to their income.

Delay in care because of having your healthcare yanked is a standard for a lot of folks who qualify and then don't qualify. Again, why do the systems we have created have to be so difficult and almost death causing?!

Meet George, "Hell no I am not going to the Emergency Room!"

George came to the clinic for his scheduled appointment looking a little scared. George, who was only a year away from Medicare, had a history of high blood pressure. When he was brought back to the exam room, vitals were done. Everything was a little on the high side. When asked how he was doing, he started to complain about some mid-level chest pain. He thought he had eaten something that did not agree with him. Our wheels started to turn. One thing led to another with the critical loops being closed. George was then on the receiving end of an EKG. Sure enough, he was actively having a heart attack. Now came the hard part, telling George he was indeed having a heart attack and he would need to go to the emergency room to address said heart attack. The first words out of his mouth were, "I can't go to the ER, I have no health insurance." Our words back to him were, "Well we can't let you go home and we don't have the equipment or the right specialists to fix your heart!" He countered by saying, "I just lost my wife, what do I really have to live for?" Our response was, "You have living family and we kind of like having you on this planet!" We bantered for a good fifteen minutes like this until he agreed to allow us to call 911 for an ambulance. As the ambulance loaded him up, he looked up into my face and simply said, "Thank you for caring about me!"

George, of course, was admitted with a whole battery of

tests run to understand how bad his heart was actually doing. Sure enough, he needed multiple stents, but did avoid any bypass surgery.

Of course, there's always a bill at the end of the procedures and admissions. He came back to the clinic with the bills in hand. We did what we always did, we helped folks navigate their way out of medical bill purgatory. George actually qualified for Medicaid.

Ironically, I was reading the local newspaper one day only to see George's picture on the obituary page. It brought me right back to that night of the heart attack. I was so happy to see George had enjoyed 10 more years of life after that fateful night. For him, that would have meant getting to spend time with his family and going to stock car races which he loved. I was reminded if we had given in to him and told him to go in the morning to be checked out, especially after all of his balking at having to go, he would have probably died in his sleep.

Instead he had those bonus years. American patients are literally scared to death to receive care because of the bill that follows! They truly opt for death by waiting until the last minute to get care! There's a lot of dialogue out there about whether healthcare is a right or a privilege. I ask this question of a lot of the youngster med students I give lectures to. Believe it or not, there are some who say it is not an American right to be given healthcare.

The truck driver who felt "health care" was for someone else!

Meet Chad, an 18-wheel tractor trailer driver. He was in need of getting his certification renewed so he would be able to drive said truck. He came through the doors, thinking it would be a slam dunk—we would sign his renewal after he peed in the cup, took his vitals, and his medical history. Only what he didn't realize or at least admit to was his blood pressure was on the high side, like 200/110 high. I could hear him mutter under his breath, "Damn!", as we delivered the news. No renewal until the blood pressure was better controlled. He stammered a bit and said, "But, it's my livelihood!" We countered with, "But it's your life and everyone's life out there while you're driving that massive truck!" He said, "I have driven past this free clinic for months, but never asked to be a patient!" I asked him to explain why he didn't stop. The next words out of his mouth made me teary, "I don't deserve to be here, this is for someone else who needs it more!" So pride kept him from coming through the doors; necessity brought him through the doors!

He was re-started on his medication that he hadn't been able to get without health insurance. He came back in a couple of weeks for a re-check of the blood pressure. With the medication, his blood pressure was nicely controlled. He was happy to be back on the medication, he had once taken. He had no idea there were discount medication lists at some of the local grocery stores and at Walmart. The medication cost him $10 for a ninety 90-day supply. $10 dollars was all that stood between him and his wellness! He was happy to have a signed renewal for his commercial driver's license (CDL). He knew that this wasn't just a one and done thing, he realized he now was cared for and by us. For him that meant stopping in on a regular basis to have his blood pressures checked. Not to mention, periodic appointments.

As I write about Chad, I am reminded that at any point in

his driving career, he could very well have had a stroke or MI and collapsed driving the huge blob of steel. What we said was true, not only could he have killed himself but whoever was in his way on the road.

Do you ever wonder while you are out driving and you see a trailer truck, is that driver healthy? Do they suffer from a chronic illness, have no health insurance, therefore they are like a time bomb waiting to happen? I am always wondering how many truck drivers have untreated sleep apnea. I will stop with the wondering but will add, it can be anyone operating a motor vehicle of any kind, who has let their health diminish because either their deductible is too high; their co-pay totals are astronomical; or they don't have any health coverage at all. **No matter the scenario, we as a country need to be better and do better!**

Social Media Influencer

Getting a call from 12-year old Molly's mother about getting her Medicaid. Medicaid is needed for what's called wraparound mental health services. Molly had tried to kill herself. Yep, you read that right, twelve and trying to get off of this planet. My first thoughts are always who is bullying them to the point they want to end their life just to be relieved of the pain. Many times kiddos will "cut" themselves to make the pain go away from the mental health demons they carry with them.

As I listened to mom relate the story of what happened to Molly, I was shocked to hear it.

Apparently, Molly was a part of a popular rock group on SnapChat. The kiddos in the group were from all over the country. Some were a little older, but none were any younger. One of the members of the group decided to put out the challenge to the others about trying to get admitted to a mental hospital. It didn't matter what they needed to do to get admitted. She decided her way in to become an inpatient was to try to commit suicide. It was around 9 or 10 in the evening. The pre-teen decided to take 'pills'. What Molly did next was to reach out to the members of the group to admit to them she had taken 'pills'. Only instead of accolades, there were crickets. No response back from anyone. Getting no response, she decided to run to her mom and admit what she had done.

Of course, she was now beyond scared and was starting to feel ill. She was whisked off to the emergency room. She was stripped and put into paper pajamas, with no underwear allowed. Since there are fewer and fewer mental health beds locally, she was going to be sent several hours away for her inpatient stay. As a twelve-year old, she bought herself an adventure she never expected to have to go through. She was separated from her family and put into an unmarked police car and driven a few hours away from the emergency room. Once there, her family was told she would have to be inpatient for a week. Her parents decided they wanted her to come back home. She did come home to a suicide proofed house. She was allowed no social media for the foreseeable future.

What has this world come to that our children are so influenced enough by a social media 'challenge', they would attempt to end their lives to be a part of that challenge?!

Are our children being bullied to the extent they have little to no self-esteem that would cause them to do harm to themselves? The resounding answer is YES! Molly was not the first young lady who attempted suicide to end the incessant bullying. As adults we allow this to continue to happen on a daily basis around the country. When do we come together to put solutions into place to save our kiddos?

Labels

Why do we apply medical labels to human beings? I would like to introduce you to Jarod. Jarod was in a motor vehicle accident in his 20's and became wheelchair bound. After trying to walk, he ended up falling multiple times to the point he required both legs to be amputated above the knees. Of course during this healthcare path, he was offered narcotics for his pain. Rightly so, who wouldn't be?! But along with those prescription narcotics came the label which would be affixed to him for the rest of his days. His label, "drug seeker" caused many problems for him. Having laid on his back for long hours and being unable to toss and turn, his spine opened up like a fileted fish. He was in such extreme pain. He and his family reached out to the medical providers to get more pain medication. Their answer was "no", you must be drug seeking. The "drug seeker" label lasted well into his last days as a forty something year old.

Ironically, he didn't make multiple trips to the ER to get medications like a lot of "drug seekers" do. Jarod had only one primary care provider. When he had to move closer to his family, he needed to find a new one. This was not an easy feat. This is where medical records are like your fingerprints, they are a part of you. There had to be a lot of advocacy to find him someone who understood his plight. With some trial and error, he finally found someone. She was a recent graduate who was afraid to get her hands slapped because she gave him "too much" of a non-narcotic medication. Jarod had to sign a contract, which indicated he would use the prescribed medication as it was written. It didn't matter he had breakthrough pain or that his caregivers had to drive miles to the pharmacy on a very frequent basis. The prescription is the prescription is the prescription. He was given a non-narcotic medication, but it was never prescribed to his pain level, so he remained in pain on a daily basis for several years. He had no ability to alleviate the pain. No matter how much he complained about the pain, the answer was always the same. You have that horrid label!

He could have sought out illicit street drugs like heroin, but he chose not to go that route and instead play by the rules.

He eventually figured out that by being in a bathtub for 18-hours a day, this would give him the most pain relief. One of the times I had a conversation with him, he was floating in his bathtub. I had joked with him about staying somewhat upright in his tub—he came back and said, "I am literally a square, it's pretty hard to go under!" His water world was set up with plants, a TV, foodstuffs, and an aquarium nearby. He never needed to worry about bodily fluids fouling the water since he had a catheter and a colostomy bag in place to catch all of them. If he came out of the water and had to be on "land", his pain level spiked to the sky. Add a ride in a car or in an ambulance, he immediately experienced pain beyond any scale that is written. If pain is based on a 1-10 scale, infinity probably wasn't an exaggeration for the pain level.

As he started to experience more and more medical issues, he found himself being an inpatient for days on end. Hospital beds - even the best of the laminar flow ones - are tough to be in for someone with this level of discomfort. He had been diagnosed with some serious issues which meant radiological follow ups. Since CT scanners are generally stationary, if he wanted to have the testing done, yep you guessed it, he had to travel by vehicle to get them done. So much pain!

He struggled on many days with the situation he was in, but had taken up writing to pass the time and to help ignore the pain. He lay in his bathtub and used his laptop to type out a large scientific/anthropological paper and then actually had started to compose a book about his life before he passed away.

Patient labels are never a good thing. The amount of delay in care experienced by Jarod was immense. The barbaric way in which he was cared for shined brightly for everyone who could 'see' him as a patient and a human. Most of the providers had to move on from 'drug seeker' in order to offer him a modicum of compassion in the form of pain management. They literally grouped him with every other labeled patient.

I believe he was owed an apology by this thing we call healthcare. He was the proverbial crème in the sandwich cookie, squeezed by both sides. He was never given a chance to raise his voice loud enough to conquer the stigma.

To Jarod, I will apologize for a system that failed you and failed you BIG time!

When in doubt, get it checked out!

Women typically have annual mammogram screenings beginning at the prescribed age. Imagine my shock, when I came across Alice with a lump the size of a grapefruit in her breast. The physician examined her. Once he was done, he said to me, "She says the lump has only been there for a couple of weeks! There is no way that lump grew that fast, it has been there for months!" Eventually she admitted that yes, the lump had been there for a long while.

She was sent for surgery to have the breast removed and to receive treatments.

The sadness in this story is she ignored getting it checked out for whatever reason, but in the end it cost her, her life. She had no idea she could have gotten a free mammogram even if uninsured. And her income was such she would have qualified for the state's Breast and Cervical Medicaid program, which would have covered her surgery and her treatments.

I go back to that adage, when in doubt, get it checked out! Her breast lump probably started out small, yet big enough she could have felt it with regular breast exams. I can't imagine what she was thinking as each day she woke up to find it was continuing to grow. The angst and scaredness she had to have felt.

This is a lesson to everyone: be proactive and understand prevention is worth its weight in gold!

Question your doctor, please!

This article was written by Michelle Berry Bingman, who was a skilled intensive care nurse at the time of its writing in 2000. She has since become a skilled nurse practitioner (CRNP). She uses her skills every day to advocate for better care for her patients in the outpatient setting located in rural America. It was published by the Press-Enterprise as an op-ed, and is reprinted here with permission. **Read and learn!**

My father recently has a second heart attack, and was for at the Berwick Hospital. It was decided he needed a heart catheterization to find out the extent of the damage. He was transferred to Wilkes-Barre General Hospital where it was performed. After the procedure the doctor told my mother that my father could not have surgery, his heart was not strong enough.

The cardiologist told my father and mother that medicines would be the only treatment. My father was started on new medicines and discharged home.

My father sought a second opinion in Harrisburg from the heart surgeon who had done his first heart surgery. The doctor agreed with the cardiologist in Wilkes-Barre.

I was at this appointment with my parents. I asked this doctor about a new procedure that was being done for persons who could not undergo a heart by-pass. This doctor had said he had heard of the procedure, but did not do the procedure. He stated that we might want to have the heart catheterization films sent to a place that did this procedure.

After being at home, my father experienced some dizziness and lightheadedness, then went to see his family doctor. She decreased and stopped some of the medicines that she thought were the cause.

A week or so passed and my father was taken to the emergency room for complaints of shortness of breath and chest pain. He was admitted again.

The partner of the cardiologist, who did my father's heart catheterization, was at the hospital the next day. It was told to my father that the medications should not be changed or stopped unless consulting with the cardiologists first. My father was found to have an irregular heartbeat and a build up of fluid around his heart.

The family doctor told my father there was nothing further they could do, she would have Hospice come in. I received a phone call at work from my mother telling me what the doctor had said. No other options were offered.

When I arrived at Berwick Hospital, my father looked as though all the life had been drained out of him. I guess anyone would look that way after being given this news by a doctor he trusted.

I asked to speak with the doctor caring for my father. The nurses in the ICU at the Berwick Hospital were wonderful, and they reached the doctor so I could speak with her.

I told her of another hospital that I thought could help my father with a procedure called the Trans-myocardial Revascularization (TMR). She told me I was grasping at straws, there was nothing that could be done, he was going to die.

When I questioned her about Hospice she stated that Hospice was a very good idea in her opinion. Hospice is for people who are dying a terminal death. My father was not a candidate for Hospice. I told her that I wanted my transferred to Washington, DC, to a hospital called Washington Hospital Center. I was told she would have to finish her treatment of my father first. In my view, she had finished her treatment, she gave him no other options, only death.

I am a cardiac surgery Registered Nurse and so this fight was not only for my father but also for all of the people area hospitals serve. I feel very lucky to have knowledge that I do. We as a society are always told, "Do what the doctor says, the doctor knows best." You are supposed to believe what the doctor tells you.

In some cases, you need to question the doctor.

On March 9, my father had coronary artery bypass surgery at Washington Hospital Center. He did not need the TMR I had spoken about; the doctor was able to give his heart blood flow that it needed with three bypasses. He recovered well after surgery and is now home, continuing to recover.

According to the doctors at the Berwick Hospital and Wilkes-Barre General Hospital, my father was not a good candidate for surgery. Just because these are small hospitals and don't want to take the risk of operating on someone doesn't mean that they need to be sent home to die. It simply means that that hospital doesn't do many heart surgeries.

There are larger hospitals in bigger cities, such as Washington Hospital Center and the Cleveland Clinic. These hospitals perform heart surgeries every day. It may seem like a factory to some, but when it comes to experience I wanted my father to be where they do this surgery routinely. Doing 15 to 30 heart surgeries a day, the doctors are very skilled.

When my father not told truthfully that Wilkes-Barre General just did not want ot take that risk, only the doctor will know. Patients should know all of their options, not just the ones the doctor sees fit. Technology is always advancing and the people in smaller communities have a right to know that there are options outside their community.

I am thankful that my parents were able to give me an education that would one day save my father's life. If left up to the doctor, who knows where my family would be right now.

I only hope this can reach other people to let them know that you need to question your doctor sometimes.

GLOSSARY

Language To Ask Better Questions!

Allowed Amount - Maximum amount on which payment is based for covered health care services. This may be called "eligible expense," "payment allowance" or "negotiated rate." If your provider charges more than the allowed amount, you may have to pay the difference. (See Balance Billing.)

Appeal - A request for your health insurer or plan to review a decision or a grievance again.

Balance Billing - When a provider bills you for the difference between the provider's charge and the allowed amount. For example, if the provider's charge is $100 and the allowed amount is $70, the provider may bill you for the remaining $30. A preferred provider may not *balance bill* you for covered services.

Co-insurance - Your share of the costs of a covered health care service, calculated as a percent (for example, 20%) of the allowed amount for the service.

For example: Jane's plan pays 80%. Jane pays 20% plus any deductibles. If the health insurance or plan's allowed amount for an office visit is $50 and you've met your deductible, your co-insurance payment of 20% would be $10. The health insurance or plan pays the rest of the allowed amount.

Complications of Pregnancy - Conditions due to pregnancy, labor and delivery that require medical care to prevent serious harm to the health of the mother or the fetus. Morning sickness and a non-emergency caesarean section aren't complications of pregnancy.

Co-payment - A fixed amount (for example, $15) you pay for a covered health care service, usually when you receive the service. The amount can vary by the type of covered health care service.

Deductible - The amount you owe for health care services your health insurance or plan covers before your health insurance or plan begins to pay. For example, if your deductible is $1000, your plan *won't pay anything* until you've met your $1000 deductible for covered health care services subject to the deductible. *The deductible may not apply to all services.*

Durable Medical Equipment (DME) - Equipment and supplies ordered by a health care provider for everyday or extended use. Coverage for DME may include: oxygen equipment, wheelchairs, crutches or blood testing strips for diabetics.

Emergency Medical Condition - An illness, injury, symptom or condition so serious that a reasonable person would seek care right away to avoid severe harm.

Emergency Medical Transportation - Ambulance services for an emergency medical condition.

Emergency Room Care - Emergency services you get in an emergency room.

Emergency Services - Evaluation of an emergency medical

condition and treatment to keep the condition from getting worse.

Excluded Services - Health care services that your health insurance or plan doesn't pay for or cover.

External Review - A process for an independent reviewer to check why a health insurer denied your coverage for services. A written request has to be made within four months of receiving the final notice of denial.

Facility Fees -A fee for outpatient services at a hospital based facility that covers the cost of providing care, i.e. keeping the lights on, buying equipment, etc. THIS FEE CAN BE APPLIED TO YOUR DEDUCTIBLE!

Grievance - A complaint that you communicate to your health insurer or plan.

Habilitation Services - Health care services that help a person keep, learn or improve skills and functioning for daily living. Examples include therapy for a child who isn't walking or talking at the expected age. These services may include physical and occupational therapy, speech-language pathology and other services for people with disabilities in a variety of inpatient and/or outpatient settings.

Health Insurance - A contract that requires your health insurer to pay some or all of your health care costs in exchange for a premium (a fee you pay).

Home Health Care - Health care services a person receives at home.

Hospice Services - Services to provide comfort and support for persons in the last stages of a terminal illness and their families.

Hospitalization - Care in a hospital that requires admission as an inpatient and usually requires an overnight stay. An overnight stay for observation could be outpatient care.

Hospital Outpatient Care - Care in a hospital that usually doesn't require an overnight stay.

In-network Co-insurance - The percent (for example, 20%) you pay of the allowed amount for covered health care services to providers who contract with your health insurance or plan. In-network co-insurance usually costs you less than out-of-network co-insurance.

In-network Co-Payment - A fixed amount (for example, $15) you pay for covered health care services to providers who contract with your health insurance or plan. In-network co-payments usually are less than out-of-network co-payments.

Medically Necessary - Health care services or supplies needed to prevent, diagnose or treat an illness, injury, condition, disease or its symptoms and that meet accepted standards of medicine.

Medicaid - a joint Federal & State insurance program designed to help people who cannot afford health insurance by paying directly for medical services rather than giving them money to pay out of pocket. Eligibility depends on income, resources, and category, and varies by state.

Medicare – A federal insurance program Medicare – primarily for 65 and older, as well as those under 65 with qualifying disabilities. Medicare covers a wide range of medically necessary services, including hospital care, doctor visits, preventive screenings, and durable medical equipment. However, it does not generally cover routine dental, vision, or hearing services, long-term custodial care, or cosmetic procedures. A beneficiary may choose *supplemental plans* or *Medicare Advantage* plans to fill these gaps.

Network - The facilities, providers and suppliers your health insurer or plan has contracted with to provide health care services.

Non-Preferred Provider - A provider who doesn't have a contract with your health insurer or plan to provide services to you. You'll pay more to see a non-preferred provider. Check your policy to see if you can go to all providers who have contracted with your health insurance or plan, or if your health insurance or plan has a **"tiered"** network and you must pay extra to see some providers.

Out-of-network Co-insurance - The percent (for example, 40%) you pay of the allowed amount for covered health care services to providers who do not contract with your health insurance or plan. Out of-network co-insurance usually costs you more than in network co-insurance.

Out-of-network Co-payment - A fixed amount (for example, $30) you pay for covered health care services from providers who do not contract with your health insurance or plan. Out-of-network co-payments usually are more than in-network co-payments.

Out-of-Pocket Limit - The most you pay during a policy period (usually a year) before your health insurance or plan begins to pay 100% of the allowed amount. This limit never includes your premium, balance-billed charges or health care your health insurance or plan doesn't cover. Some health insurance or plans don't count all of your co-payments, deductibles, co-insurance payments, out-of-network payments or other expenses toward this limit.

Physician Services - Health care services which a licensed medical physician (M.D. – Medical Doctor or D.O. – Doctor of Osteopathic Medicine) provides or coordinates.

Plan Provider - A benefit your employer, union or other group sponsor provides to you to pay for your health care services.

Preauthorization - A decision by your health insurer or plan that a health care service, treatment plan, prescription drug or durable medical equipment is medically necessary. Sometimes called prior authorization, prior approval or precertification. Your health insurance or plan may require preauthorization for certain services before you receive them, except in an emergency. Preauthorization isn't a promise your health insurance or plan will cover the cost.

Preferred Provider - A provider who has a contract with your health insurer or plan to provide services to you at a discount. Check your policy to see if you can see all preferred providers or if your health insurance or plan has a "tiered" network and you must pay extra to see some providers. Your health insurance or plan may have preferred providers who are also "participating" providers. Participating providers also contract with your health insurer or plan, but the discount may not be as great, and you may have to pay more.

Premium - The amount that must be paid for your health insurance or plan. You and/or your employer usually pay it monthly, quarterly or yearly.

Prescription Drug Coverage - Health insurance or plan that helps pay for prescription drugs and medications.

Prescription Drugs - Drugs and medications that by law require a prescription.

Primary Care Physician - A physician (M.D. – Medical Doctor or D.O. – Doctor of Osteopathic Medicine) who directly provides or coordinates a range of health care services for a patient.

Primary Care Provider - A physician (M.D. – Medical Doctor or D.O. – Doctor of Osteopathic Medicine), nurse practitioner, clinical nurse specialist or physician assistant, as allowed under state law, who provides, coordinates or helps a patient access a range of health care services.

Professional Fees - A charge for any services provided typically by a physician or other healthcare provider.

Provider - A physician (M.D. – Medical Doctor or D.O. – Doctor of Osteopathic Medicine), health care professional or health care facility licensed, certified or accredited as required by state law.

Reconstructive Surgery - Surgery and follow-up treatment needed to correct or improve a part of the body because of birth defects, accidents, injuries or medical conditions.

Rehabilitation Services - Health care services that help a person keep, get back or improve skills and functioning for daily living that have been lost or impaired because a person was sick, hurt or disabled. These services may include physical and occupational therapy, speech-language pathology and psychiatric rehabilitation services in a variety of inpatient and/or outpatient settings.

Skilled Nursing Care - Services from licensed nurses in your own home or in a nursing home. Skilled care services are from technicians and therapists in your own home or in a nursing home.

Specialist - A physician specialist focuses on a specific area of medicine or a group of patients to diagnose, manage, prevent or treat certain types of symptoms and conditions. A non-physician specialist is a provider who has more training in a specific area of health care.

Surprise Billing - The *No Surprises Act* protects patients from unexpected medical bills for care received at emergency rooms and other facilites.

UCR (Usual Customary and Reasonable) - The amount paid for a medical service in a geographic area based on what providers in the area usually charge for the same or similar medical service. The UCR amount sometimes is used to determine the allowed amount.

Urgent Care - Care for an illness, injury or condition serious enough that a reasonable person would seek care right away, but not so severe as to require emergency room care.

VA/Tricare - a federal health care program run by the Department of Defense that provides coverage for active-duty service members, military retirees, their families, and certain survivors. It is not private insurance and operates under federal law with uniform national standards, meaning benefits are consistent across all states.

ABOUT THE AUTHOR

Bette A. Grey

Bette Anderson Grey, BA, RRT, CPFT has over 40 years of experience in the healthcare field, including being a respiratory therapist; having worked in many different healthcare arenas, from a trauma unit to outpatient medical services. She is extremely passionate about patient lives having started a free medical clinic for the working uninsured known as Columbia County Volunteers In Medicine Clinic in rural Pennsylvania.

She has served in multiple local and state capacities, including PA State Boards of Medicine, hospital safety committees, and as a member of the PA Society for Respiratory Care.

BOOKS BY THIS AUTHOR

Death Is Not An Option: A View From A Free Medical Clinic

A true and often harrowing account of Bette Grey's founding of the Columbia County Volunteers in Medicine Clinic, Inc. in Berwick, PA. It depicts the tragic and heartwarming accounts of patients at the clinic.

This free clinic continues to be in operation today.

www.ingramcontent.com/pod-product-compliance
Lightning Source LLC
La Vergne TN
LVHW100347150926
847902LV00024B/181
* 9 7 9 8 9 9 6 9 2 5 6 7 4 *